PICTURING SCOTLAND

CAITHNESS &
SUTHERLAND

NESS PUBLISHING

2   A view to prove Scotland's mountains don't have to be above the magic 3000ft (914m) contour to be impressive and challenging in equal measure. This is Quinag, a huge triple-topped pile

CAITHNESS & SUTHERLAND

that begins north of Loch Assynt. This is its western ridge, with the summit of Spidean Coinich (764m/2506ft), one of the three tops, on the right.

Welcome to Caithness & Sutherland!

Among the many worlds of Scotland, the northernmost part of the realm is indeed a place apart. Many of those who come under its spell go further in their descriptions, referring to it as a 'lunar' landscape; when someone tells you that while Scotland as a whole is unique, some parts of it are more unique than others – it is Caithness and Sutherland of which they speak. But before we get too carried away, it is important to remember that they were two distinct counties. They became joined in political terms due to their forming a single parliamentary constituency from 1918 to 1997. Very different in character, Caithness is a wide-open world that embraces the peat-land 'Flow Country' on the one hand and fertile agricultural plains on the other, while Sutherland is a land of wilderness and extraordinarily shaped mountains, one of the least-populated parts of Western Europe.

One thing Sutherland and Caithness share is an abundance of water, stored in countless lochs and lochans, flowing through endless burns and rivers. The surrounding seas have created (and of course are continually modifying) a most dramatic coastline, producing legions of towering cliffs, sea stacks, caves and arches. This process has been accentuated by the land having risen since the last Ice Age. So, although Caithness is lower lying than Sutherland, it shares these coastal features, with much of its landscape coming to an abrupt halt, high above the sea. Mankind's influence is far more noticeable on the eastern seaboard, where a coastal strip has

4

Sutherland winter evening: looking west across the northern end of Loch Shin to the Ben More **5**
Assynt massif, the highest point in the county with a summit of 998m/3274ft.

allowed the development of farming, and where inlets and estuaries have provided natural harbours for the fishing fleets. Sadly, this is also an area where man's inhumanity to man has been practiced in the Clearances that swept people away in favour of more profitable commodities. Those who eked out an already marginal living through subsistence farming were evicted to the remote coastal margins where they were expected to adapt to even greater adversity. Many did not stop at the coast, but took shipping for yet more distant lands. Much evidence of this period remains, as we shall see.

The starting point of this book's journey is Dornoch, Sutherland's delightful county town. With a history that goes back a thousand years, it has been the religious and administrative centre of Sutherland for 800 years. In a way, Dornoch seems out of place: northern Scotland is not supposed (is it?) to offer a town of such cosy charm that might be more anticipated on, say, the Galloway coast at the other end of the country. But that is a big part of its appeal,

6   Dornoch's drinking fountain, presented by Miss Georgina Anderson in 1892.

the surprise of this tucked-away haven just where one might not expect to find such a place.

From Dornoch we travel clockwise around the region, which initially means heading north-west across Sutherland over to its western coast, then weaving hither and thither up to the far north. There we turn east and head into Caithness, home of the most northerly point on the Scottish mainland. The final leg is down the east coast with one or two explorations inland. This is the part of the journey that takes in several of the abundance of ancient ritual sites, some of which go right back to Neolithic times. The sheer range of scenery, wildlife and built landscape add up to a unique experience courtesy of a unique land. And, if that's not enough, this part of Scotland is quite often treated to one of nature's most extraordinary phenomena, the Northern Lights (see back cover).

Plenty to do in Dornoch: the signpost points to the beach, the witch's stone, the golf course and more.

8   Dornoch Square is a gracious and fitting centre for a Royal Burgh, the status it was granted in 1628. The run of buildings from left to centre of the picture includes Dornoch Jail, The Courthouse

and Dornoch Castle, which was never actually a castle, but built as the Bishop's Palace in the 16th century. Today it is a hotel.

10 Dornoch High Street seen from the Cathedral churchyard. Part of Dornoch's charm is the survival of traditional, independent shops such as the chemist on the right. There's a bookshop too!

To quote from a local website, 'There are grander cathedrals than Dornoch, but few so immediately **11** captivate the human soul. The red sandstone building exudes life and love.'

12 Gilbert of Moravia, Bishop of Caithness, founded Dornoch Cathedral in 1224. It has had a turbulent history and required major restoration work from 1835 to 1837. This is the East Window.

In totally contrasting style, this beautiful glasswork is a detail from the window donated by the 13 widow of Stewart Anderson, a former organist of Dornoch Cathedral.

14 Dornoch beach boasts both soft sand and rockier areas. It is so extensive that it can be seen from miles away on the south side of the Dornoch Firth.

Dornoch is a world-renowned golfing venue. The Royal Dornoch Golf Course, designed by Old Tom **15** Morris from St Andrews, is synonymous with some of the most famous names in the game.

16 Moving on from Dornoch, this viewpoint is on the south side of the Dornoch Firth in Easter Ross, but provides a good place from which to set the scene for what lies ahead. The distant snow-covered

mountain (opposite page) is Ben Klibreck, 28 miles to the north. Above, the north-west view takes in the Dornoch Firth, with Ben More Assynt rising 30 miles beyond.

18 The village of Bonar Bridge is situated at the head of the Dornoch Firth and until recent times was the lowest bridging point. The shape of the bridge is matched by the shapes of the clouds.

Looking downstream, more reflections and some brilliant autumn colour. Back in the pre-bridge **19** days of 1809, an overloaded ferry capsized near here, with the loss of 99 lives.

20 A few miles north of Bonar Bridge the River Shin thunders over spectacular waterfalls in a deep gorge. Inset: a salmon leaping up the falls.

To the north again is the village of Lairg, seen in the distance in this view from Ord Hill. The stones in the foreground are remains of a Neolithic chambered tomb dating from about 3000BC.

22 The largest area of fresh water in Caithness and Sutherland is Loch Shin which stretches 17 miles northwards from Lairg. This view shows the landscape and land use around the loch near Lairg.

Next comes a short westerly hop over to Rosehall in Strath Oykel, specifically at Invercassley where 23 the River Cassley (above) joins the Oykel. There is good trout and salmon fishing here.

24 A misty autumn dawn in Strath Oykel. As the mixed farming that can be seen suggests, this is fertile land. Norse invaders discovered its potential and drove out the Gaels who were living here then.

The name 'Oykel' is derived from the Norse *Ekkjal*. Strath Oykel is the traditional boundary between Ross-shire (to the south) and Sutherland.

26 The introduction referred to Sutherland's extraordinary mountains and Suilven (731m/2398ft), seen here in the process of creating a cloud, is probably the most dramatic of all.

From the head of Strath Oykel by Loch Craggie, just a few minutes later the cloud has grown **27** considerably. The mountain may now be shrouded but the overall composition is a delight.

28 From a spot near where the previous picture was taken, but looking north instead of north-west, rolls of early-morning mist fill the foreground, above which Ben More Assynt rears into view.

In contrast to the slightly coy glimpse of Ben More Assynt opposite, here it stands proud in winter **29** glory, with the village of Elphin in the foreground – all in all, a classic Sutherland scene.

30 A few miles further north at Inchnadamph, a wind-blown pine tree provides the perfect framing for Quinag, with its Spidean Coinich summit on the left and Sail Garbh summit to its right.

Inchnadamph is at the eastern end of Loch Assynt where, on its promontory (virtually an island), **31** also stands Ardvreck Castle, 15th-century seat of the MacLeods of Assynt.

32 The view back to the south from Ardvreck includes Conival, Ben More Assynt's secondary Munro (Scottish mountains above 914m/3000ft) top, seen here at the right-hand end of the snowy ridge.

Left: Loch Assynt has numerous tree-filled islets near its shores. Right: Red Deer are abundant throughout the north of Scotland and the stags are always an impressive sight.

34 A scene which characterises Loch Assynt, where remnants of the Caledonian pine forest cling to the rocky shores. The rock face in the background ascends almost vertically . . .

. . . as it forms the lower part of Quinag's western elevation, that fearsome spectacle first seen on **35** pages 2-3 and a close-up of which we can study here.

36 The road along Loch Assynt goes to Lochinver, Sutherland's largest west-coast settlement, where the harbour is still busy. This quiet evening view shows how the village is wrapped around the loch.

Being on the west coast it is of course ideally placed to catch lovely sunsets. In the foreground is the **37** mouth of the River Inver, which flows down from Loch Assynt.

38 Pushing on ever further up provides the chance to see the northern aspect of Quinag, which looks nothing like the previous views. But that's part of the fascination of these mountains.

The sea lochs which extend, fjord-like, miles inland either add many miles to the journey or require **39** a ferry, as was the case here at Kylesku. This impressive bridge was opened in 1984.

40 The road network peters out in the far north-west, meaning some of the best locations can only be reached on foot or by boat. Sandwood Bay is a prime example. Often described as the most

magnificent beach in the UK, this picture supports that notion. The fact that it requires a four-mile walk from Blairmore only adds to the enjoyment by adding a sense of achievement.

42 Returning a little to the south, Badcall Bay demonstrates a different face of the coast, where a pattern of islands and skerries adds interest and fires the imagination – just what *is* out there?

Part of the answer is wildlife, including a huge variety of seabirds – you might see a Black-throated **43** Diver like this one. Handa Island Nature Reserve is not far from here.

44 Next we take a south-easterly detour to see the mountains around Loch Stack. Above is Meall Liath Coire Mhic Dhughaill (801m/2628ft) – the longest name of any mountain in the Highlands!

Turn 90° to the left and, in the last light of a winter afternoon, stands Arkle (787m/2582ft), perfectly **45**
reflected in the partly frozen loch.

46 The north coast of Sutherland is reached at the village of Durness, location of the amazing Smoo Cave. Above is the entrance to this huge limestone cavern, the most dramatic coastline cave in Britain.

Inside, it is even more spectacular, with a large waterfall cascading through the roof. Visitors can take a boat ride into the illuminated depths of the cavern.

48 Heading east out of Durness, it's just a short distance to this idyllic beach at Sangobeg.
The Clearances in this area were met with some resistance, requiring a degree of military support.

The lengthy sea inlet of Loch Eriboll used to have a ferry before the building of the road. The **49** promontory of Ard Neakie, seen here, was its eastern terminus, where disused limekilns also remain.

50 OK, a bit of a cliché picture, but plenty of Highland Cattle are to be seen in this area. These are by the road that runs south along Loch Hope on the way to our next stop, Ben Hope.

On a day like this, the start point of the path up Ben Hope is a most perfect spot. If camping here, **51** use the waterfalls as a shower! The summit (927m/3041ft) can just be seen.

52 Ben Hope is the most northerly of the Munros and provides grandstand views in all directions. About 10 miles to the west is mighty Foinaven, with its treacherous switchback ridge.

Turning to the north, Loch Hope is the nearer stretch of water, while beyond is Loch Eriboll – Ard **53** Neakie (page 49) can just be made out on the extreme left of the picture.

54 Brochs are among Scotland's most impressive Iron Age buildings. Dun Dornaigil is a well-preserved example near Ben Hope, which can be seen on the right of the picture.

East of Ben Hope and south of Tongue is Ben Loyal, another flight of improbable fancy in the **55** mountain-building stakes! This is its north face, seen from the Kyle of Tongue Causeway.

56 During the ascent of Ben Loyal, the views soon begin to open up. Patches of sunlight illuminate the village of Tongue and bring a green tint to the sea. Ben Loyal is not a great height at 764m/2506ft,

but the variety and number of the individual tops mean there is plenty to explore.

58 The summit of Ben Loyal is named An Caisteal (the Castle). Left: sizing up the task of getting to the top. Right: the climb in progress. (The rock climb is not the only way up!)

The reward for the climb: wilderness stretches away to the east. Ptarmigan inhabit the Sutherland 59 mountain tops. Their summer plumage helps them blend in with the rocks. Inset: female Ptarmigan.

60 Left: male Ptarmigan (with orange eye stripe) on Ben Loyal. Right: Back on the north coast near Bettyhill, the Pictish 'Farr Stone' stands outside Strathnaver Museum.

A storm approaches Farr Bay. In the 'storm' of the Clearances, many people from Strath Naver came **61** to Bettyhill, which can be seen in the distance. Ben Loyal is just visible on the skyline.

62 Rough weather can add to the excitement of Caithness and Sutherland as the rapidly changing patterns of light on a stormy day can add drama to the wilderness, as here at Loch Badanloch.

This aerial view of Melvich (between Bettyhill and Thurso) provides a last look at Sutherland's north **63** coast, summing it up: beach, cliffs, fertile coastal strip, inland wilderness, distant mountains.

64 And so to Caithness, where we arrive at Thurso, Scotland's most northerly town. The central focus of the town is Sir John's Square, with St Peter's & St Andrew's Church beyond.

East of Thurso in the village of Dunnet is Mary Ann's Cottage, former home of Mary Ann Calder **65** who lived here for over 90 years. Its preservation provides a window on crofting life of times past.

66 Dunnet Head is the most northerly point on the mainland of Scotland. The Lighthouse was designed by Robert Stevenson and built in 1831. The Orkney island of Hoy lies in the distance.

The spectacular 100m/330ft cliffs of Dunnet Head are seen here from near the Castle of Mey, a few miles to the east. The harvest is in and those round hay bales make a pleasing foreground.

68 The Castle of Mey was bought by the Queen Mother in 1952 following the death of her husband, King George VI. Immaculately maintained, it is her lasting legacy to Caithness.

The Dining Room at the Castle of Mey. The Queen Mother used to sit at the near end of the table. **69**
The whole of the interior is a wonderful period piece which reflects the era of her ownership.

70 The Walled Garden at the Castle of Mey is separated into sections by mixed hedges, both to work as windbreaks and to create surprises around each corner, such as the Shell Rose Garden seen here.

Canisbay Kirk is a short distance east of the Castle of Mey and is where the Queen Mother **71** worshipped while staying there. The church contains a plaque to her memory.

72 Coastal erosion makes for much spectacular scenery, such as here at Duncansby Head to the east of John o'Groats where there are many rock stacks to behold. Inset: Puffins are a great favourite among

the seabird population of the area. They can be seen from May to July. This one has a beak full of sand eels, their favoured diet.

74 John o'Groats has built a reputation for being at the extreme north-eastern corner of the UK mainland, 874 miles from Land's End in the extreme south-west, making it a magnet for tourists.

Now heading south, the appeal of the 'minimalist' harbour at Staxigoe, just outside Wick, is that it 75 must have looked pretty much like this back in the times of the Norse incomers who named it.

76 A few miles north of Wick, the remains of 14th-century Castle Sinclair Girnigoe are a scheduled monument and it is the only castle in Scotland to be listed by the World Monuments Fund.

To the south of Wick (County Town of Caithness), the Old Castle of Wick stands in a similar type of location to Castle Sinclair Girnigoe – each one highly defensible above rocky 'goes' or inlets.

78 Even the most inconvenient harbours have been used by fishing boats, notably Whaligoe Haven south of Wick, to which a fearsome flight of about 360 steps was constructed over 200 years ago.

Inland from Ulbster is Cairn o'Get, a burial tomb that has been a feature of the landscape for 5,000 years. It is surrounded by prehistoric remains spanning thousands of years of human activity.

80 Loch Watenen, also near Ulbster, typifies the landscape of much of inland Caithness, where a patchwork of small lochs provides the ideal habitat for all manner of wetland wildlife.

At 69.5m/228ft long, the reconstructed Camster Long Cairn shows us Neolithic architecture on a **81** grand scale. It may have begun as a pair of round cairns or may have been built as we see it now.

82 Away to the west of Camster, the unusual horseshoe stone setting at Achavanich is open on the south-east side and may never have been a complete oval. Today, 36 out of perhaps 60 stones remain.

Laidhay Croft Museum is housed in a two-hundred-year-old, rush-thatched Caithness longhouse **83** north of Dunbeath which shows how people lived and worked in the 18th and 19th centuries.

84 Spectacular or precarious? The setting of Dunbeath Castle could be thought of as either! However, as it has stood there for about 550 years, its location must be more stable than it looks.

From Dunbeath, an inland detour to Braemore where an active croft is in the foreground, backed by **85** an attractive scattering of Scots pines with the rocky but shapely Maiden Pap rising beyond.

86 A dark picture to represent dark times: Badbea is the haunting site of a long-abandoned settlement. During the Clearances, people were uprooted from the fertile straths inland and forced to live here.

The plight of the cleared peoples is evocatively captured in this statue named 'The Emigrants' a few **87** miles down the road in Helmsdale. They look in opposite directions – past and future.

88 Aside from 'The Emigrants', Helmsdale is a pleasing town in a beautiful setting by the mouth of the river of the same name. There has been a settlement here since Viking times and probably before then.

The story of the town and area is told at Timespan Museum & Arts Centre which is housed in the long building immediately to the right of the bridge.

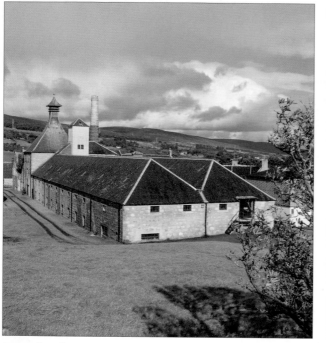
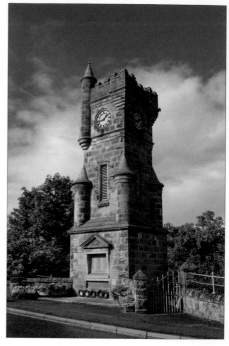

90 Left: a few miles on is Brora, home of Clynelish Distillery. It is a modern distillery; this is the old building, no longer producing the whisky. Right: Brora's impressive, castellated War Memorial.

If there were a prize for the most 'fairytale' castle in Scotland, Dunrobin would be the winner.
Although it goes back to the 13th century, what is seen today dates to the mid 1800s.

92 There is much French influence (e.g. the conical spires) blended in with the Scottish Baronial style. The garden, part of which is seen here, is based on those at the Palace of Versailles.

Falconry displays are an exciting aspect of a visit to Dunrobin and many birds of prey, such as this **93**
magnificent golden eagle, can be admired at close quarters.

94 Seals can often be seen basking on sandbanks or rocks, sometimes quite close to shore. These are taking it easy at low tide on Loch Fleet, a little to the north of Dornoch.

Websites and phone numbers (where available) for principal places featured in this book in alphabetical order:

Achavanich Stones: www.caithnessarchaeology.org.uk/achavanich
Assynt: www.assynt.info
Cairn o'Get: www.historic-scotland.gov.uk (T) 01667 460232
Caithness & Sutherland: www.letsgonorth.com
Caithness: www.caithness.org
Camster Cairns: www.historic-scotland.gov.uk (T) 01667 460232
Canisbay Kirk: www.canisbaychurch.org
Castle of Mey: www.castleofmey.org.uk (T) 01847 851473
Castle Sinclair Girnigoe: www.castlesinclairgirnigoe.org
Clynelish Distillery: www.diageo.com (T) 01408 623000
Dornoch Bookshop: www.visitdornoch.com (T) 01862 810165
Dornoch Cathedral: www.dornoch-cathedral.com
Dornoch: www.visitdornoch.com
Dun Dornaigil Broch: www.historic-scotland.gov.uk
Dunbeath Castle and Estate: www.dunbeath.co.uk (T) 01593 731308
Dunrobin Castle: www.dunrobincastle.co.uk (T) 01408 633177
Durness: www.durness.org
Falls of Shin: www.fallsofshin.co.uk/ (T) 01549 402231
Handa Island Reserve: www.scottishwildlifetrust.org.uk (T) 0131 312 7765
Laidhay Croft Museum: www.laidhay.co.uk (T) 07563 702321
Lairg and Loch Shin: www.lairg.org.uk
Loch Fleet Reserve: www.scottishwildlifetrust.org.uk/reserve/loch-fleet (T) 0131 312 7765
Maps of Caithness and Sutherland: www.scottish-places.info/counties
Old Pulteney Distillery: www.oldpulteney.com (T) 01955 602371

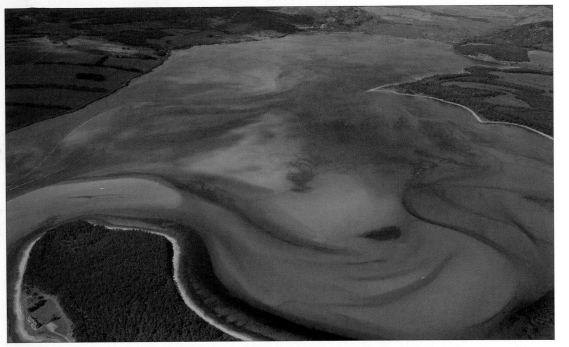

Our journey has come full circle, so let's finish on a high note by way of this aerial view of Loch Fleet, which gives a unique perspective on this lovely tidal basin. **95**

Published 2013 by Ness Publishing, 47 Academy Street, Elgin, Moray, IV30 1LR
Phone 01343 549663 www.nesspublishing.co.uk

All photographs © Colin Nutt except pp. 1, 4, 43 & 73 © Laurie Campbell; p.33 (right) © Sue M. Cleave;
pp. 63, 95 & back cover © Scotavia Images

Text © Colin Nutt
ISBN 978-1-906549-21-3

Front cover: Ardvreck Castle, Loch Assynt; p.1: common sundew; p.4: Puffin;
this page: at Pulteney Distillery, Wick; back cover: Northern Lights

For a list of websites and phone numbers please turn over > > > >

Our journey has come full circle, so let's finish on a high note by way of this aerial view of Loch **95** Fleet, which gives a unique perspective on this lovely tidal basin.

Published 2013 by Ness Publishing, 47 Academy Street, Elgin, Moray, IV30 1LR
Phone 01343 549663   www.nesspublishing.co.uk

ISBN 978-1-906549-21-3

Front cover: Ardvreck Castle, Loch Assynt; p.1: common sundew; p.4: Puffin;
this page: at Pulteney Distillery, Wick; back cover: Northern Lights

For a list of websites and phone numbers please turn over > > > >

Websites and phone numbers (where available) for principal places featured in this book in alphabetical order:

Achavanich Stones: www.caithnessarchaeology.org.uk/achavanich
Assynt: www.assynt.info
Cairn o'Get: www.historic-scotland.gov.uk (T) 01667 460232
Caithness & Sutherland: www.letsgonorth.com
Caithness: www.caithness.org
Camster Cairns: www.historic-scotland.gov.uk (T) 01667 460232
Canisbay Kirk: www.canisbaychurch.org
Castle of Mey: www.castleofmey.org.uk (T) 01847 851473
Castle Sinclair Girnigoe: www.castlesinclairgirnigoe.org
Clynelish Distillery: www.diageo.com (T) 01408 623000
Dornoch Bookshop: www.visitdornoch.com (T) 01862 810165
Dornoch Cathedral: www.dornoch-cathedral.com
Dornoch: www.visitdornoch.com
Dun Dornaigil Broch: www.historic-scotland.gov.uk
Dunbeath Castle and Estate: www.dunbeath.co.uk (T) 01593 731308
Dunrobin Castle: www.dunrobincastle.co.uk (T) 01408 633177
Durness: www.durness.org
Falls of Shin: www.fallsofshin.co.uk/ (T) 01549 402231
Handa Island Reserve: www.scottishwildlifetrust.org.uk (T) 0131 312 7765
Laidhay Croft Museum: www.laidhay.co.uk (T) 07563 702321
Lairg and Loch Shin: www.lairg.org.uk
Loch Fleet Reserve: www.scottishwildlifetrust.org.uk/reserve/loch-fleet (T) 0131 312 7765
Maps of Caithness and Sutherland: www.scottish-places.info/counties
Old Pulteney Distillery: www.oldpulteney.com (T) 01955 602371